AMERICAN HOME'S

LEARN TO COOK BOOK

CHILTON BOOK COMPANY

Philadelphia   New York   London

By VIRGINIA T. HABEEB,
Food and Equipment Editor, American Home,
and FRANCES M. CRAWFORD,
Associate Food Editor, American Home

Copyright © 1970 by Chilton Book Company
Published in Philadelphia by Chilton Book Company
and simultaneously in Ontario, Canada,
by Thomas Nelson & Sons, Ltd.

Second printing, January 1970

SBN: 8019 5567 X   *Paper Edition*
SBN: 8019 5568 8   *Cloth Edition*

Manufactured in the United States of America

INTRODUCTION

The best way to learn to cook is to jump right in with ingredients, utensils, aprons and all and start to cook. That's what this book is all about. Whether you're a beginner who hasn't learned basic techniques, an experienced cook who has forgotten them, or one who never really learned "why" you do things a certain way, you'll want to follow these easy step-by-step directions and get sure-fire results. By popular demand we offer these recipes for cooks of all ages. Here is a collection of our popular LEARNING TO COOK series which continues to run monthly in the pages of AMERICAN HOME.

CONTENTS

CHAPTER I   BREADS

Biscuits   1
Jam Muffins   2
Basic Roll Dough   3
      Pan Rolls   5
      Parker House Rolls   5
      Easy Clovers   5

CHAPTER II   EGGS

Hard-cooked Eggs   6
Soft-cooked Eggs   6
Fluffy Scrambled Eggs   7
The French Omelet   8

CHAPTER III   BEVERAGES

Cocoa 10
Coffee 11
Tea 11

CHAPTER IV

Rice 12

CHAPTER V   MAIN DISHES

Oven Fried Chicken 14
Creole Pork Chops 15
Macaroni Frankfurter Casserole 16
Tuna Florentine 17
Spaghetti and Meatballs 18
Stuffed Eggs au Gratin 20
Meatball Pizza 21
Roast Stuffed Turkey 24
Old-Fashioned Meat Loaf 27

CHAPTER VI   SALADS

Chicken Cranberry Salad 28
Tossed Cheese and Cracker Salad 31

CHAPTER VII   CAKES

Butter Cakes—Busy Day Cake 32
Foam Cakes—Sponge Cupcakes 35
Easter Lamb Cake 36

Miniature Fruit Cakes 38

CHAPTER VIII   FROSTINGS AND FILLING
Lemon Fluff Frosting 39
Favorite Chocolate Frosting 39
Vanilla Sauce 40

CHAPTER IX   PIES
Strawberry Velvet Pie 41
Caramel Apple Pie 43

CHAPTER X   COOKIES
Old-Fashioned Sugar Cookies 44
Ginger Cookies 45
        Gingerbread Men 46

CHAPTER XI   DESSERTS
Apple Betty 47
Dutch Peach Cake 48
Soft Custard 50
Golden Baked Custard 50
Old-Fashioned Rice Pudding 51
Cream Puffs 52
        Pastry Cream 53
        Chocolate Glaze 54
Strawberry Cloud 54

CHAPTER XII   CONFECTIONS
Tips on Candy Making 56
Peanut Brittle 56
Chocolate Cherries 57
Popcorn Balls 58
Walnut Butterscotch Candy Balls 59
Peanut Butter Fudge 60
Nut Mints 60
Spiced Nuts 61
Apricot Pineapple Jam 62

HELPFUL INFORMATION 63

BREADS

ROLLED BISCUITS

2 cups sifted all-purpose flour
3 teaspoons baking powder
1 teaspoon salt
¼ cup shortening
¾ cup milk

. Set out two 8-inch-round cake pans.

. Sift flour, baking powder, and salt into
medium-size mixing bowl.

. Add shortening. Cut in with pastry
blender until mixture is crumbly.

. Add almost all the milk. Stir with fork
until mixture holds together and forms a
ball. If you must add more milk, do it

gradually. Too much milk will make the
dough sticky, not enough milk will make
the biscuits dry.

5. Turn dough onto lightly floured board.
Roll ball around 3 or 4 times.

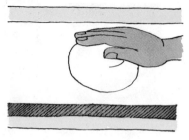

6. Knead lightly and quickly by folding
the back end to the front, pressing down,
then turning dough a quarter the way
around. Knead 20 times to smooth dough.

7. Dust a rolling pin lightly with flour. Roll
out dough to ½" thickness.

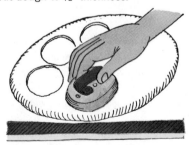

8. Cut out biscuits with 2-inch-round cutter. Dip cutter into flour before cutting
each biscuit. Cut biscuits close together.
Remove the pieces of dough in between
the biscuits, leaving biscuits in place on
the board. Reroll the pieces later.

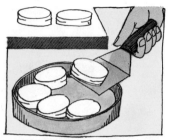

9. Pick up biscuits with spatula and put close together in pans. Put in 450° oven. Bake 15 minutes or until golden. Serve hot. Makes 16 to 18.

3. Beat the egg slightly with a fork in medium-size bowl.

4. Measure the milk and stir into the egg Measure and stir in the oil or melte and cooled shortening.

JAM MUFFINS

1 egg
1 cup milk
¼ cup pure vegetable oil or cooled, melted shortening
2 cups sifted all-purpose flour
¼ cup sugar
3 teaspoons baking powder
1 teaspoon salt
12 teaspoons strawberry jam

1. Heat oven to 400° F.

2. Grease just the bottoms of twelve 2¾-inch muffin-pan cups. Or, put paper baking cups into the pan.

5. Put the sifted flour, sugar, baking powder, and salt into a sifter. Sift the dry ingredients directly into the egg mixture

6. Stir only until the dry ingredients are moistened. The batter should be lumpy. The secret of good muffins is not to bea the batter—just stir it.

. Fill each muffin cup one third full. rop a teaspoonful of strawberry jam on ne center of the batter in each cup. Add atter to each cup to fill it two thirds full.

. Bake 20 to 25 minutes or until golden rown. Muffins will have gently rounded ops and will look pebbly rather than mooth.

. Remove from oven. Place on wire rack. oosen muffins immediately with a small patula. Serve warm. Makes 1 dozen.

BASIC ROLL DOUGH

1⅓ cups milk
⅓ cup sugar
1½ teaspoons salt
½ cup shortening
½ cup warm water (105° to 115°F.)
2 packages active dry yeast or
2 cakes compressed yeast
2 eggs
7 cups (about) sifted all-purpose flour

1. Combine milk, sugar, salt, and shortening in medium-size saucepan.

2. Heat just until tiny bubbles appear around the edge of milk mixture. This indicates the milk has reached the scalding point.

3. Remove from heat. Let mixture cool to lukewarm. To test for the right temperature, drop a small amount on the inside of the wrist. Liquid should feel neither warm nor cold. If you use a thermometer the temperature should be 90° to 95° F.

4. Measure warm water into a large, warm mixing bowl. Sprinkle or crumble in yeast. Stir to dissolve.

5. Stir in lukewarm milk mixture. Stir in eggs.

6. Add 4 cups flour. Beat smooth.

7. Mix in enough of the remaining flour until dough pulls away from sides of bowl. It will be sticky.

8. Sprinkle board with some of the remaining flour. Turn dough out of bowl onto board.

9. Work flour from board into dough with a spatula until it is stiff enough to handle.

10. Flour hands lightly. Press dough out flat. Pick up edge of dough farthest from you and fold it over the top to bring to edge nearest you.

11. Push dough away from you with the heels of your hands. Press dough lightly and use a rocking motion as you push. Turn dough one quarter the way around on the board.

12. Repeat steps 10 and 11 until dough is smooth and elastic. It takes about 5 minutes. Kneaded dough will look full and rounded, with tiny bubbles just under surface. Dough will not stick to board or hands.

13. Put dough in large, greased bowl. Turn dough over to bring greased side to top. This helps top to stay soft and stretch easily as it rises.

14. Cover the bowl with a clean towel. Set in a warm place (85° F.), free from draft, 1½ hours or until dough is doubled in bulk.

15. To test for double in bulk: Press tips of two fingers quickly and lightly about a half inch into dough. If mark remains, dough is double. If dent fills in at once, dough needs more time. Let it rise 10 minutes and test it again.

16. Punch dough down. Push your fist in the center and pull edges from sides to center. Turn ball of dough over. Cover; let rise about 30 minutes or until almost double.

17. Punch dough down again. Turn out on board. Knead just enough to distribute the air bubbles. Divide and shape according to one of the directions below.

18. Heat oven to 400° F.

19. Cover rolls with clean towel. Let rise about 20 minutes or until doubled in bulk.

20. Bake 15 to 20 minutes.

SHAPING ROLLS

PAN ROLLS

1. Divide Roll Dough into three pieces.

2. Shape each piece into a rope 12 inches long. Cut each rope into 12 equal-size pieces. Shape each piece into a smooth ball.

3. Place about ¼ inch apart in greased 9-inch layer-cake pans.

PARKER HOUSE ROLLS

1. Divide Roll Dough into three pieces.

2. Roll out each piece to a 9-inch circle. Cut into rounds with 2½-inch cookie cutter.

3. Make a crease in each round with the dull edge of a knife just to one side of the center. Brush lightly with melted butter or margarine.

4. Fold larger side over smaller one so edges just meet. Press to seal.

5. Place 1 inch apart on greased cookie sheets.

EASY CLOVERS

1. Divide Roll Dough into three pieces.

2. Shape each piece into a rope 12 inches long. Cut each rope into 12 equal-size pieces. Form each piece into a ball.

3. Place in greased muffin-pan cups.

4. Cut each ball in half with scissors, then into quarters, cutting almost to bottom of ball. Brush lightly with melted butter or margarine.

EGGS

HARD COOKED EGGS

THE COLD-WATER METHOD

1. Put eggs in saucepan and add enough water so it is 1 inch above the eggs.

2. Place over heat and bring to boiling rapidly.

3. As soon as the water boils, turn off heat or remove pan from unit or burner to prevent further cooking.

4. Cover pan and let eggs stand in water 15 minutes.

5. Cool the eggs promptly in cold water. This prevents further cooking, which is so important if you want to avoid hav-ing a discolored egg yolk. It also makes it easier to remove the shells.

BOILING WATER METHOD

1. Put enough water into saucepan to cover eggs (but do not put eggs in pan).

2. To avoid cracked shells let eggs stand in bowl of warm water. Bring water in pan to boiling. Transfer eggs with a spoon.

3. Reduce heat to keep water below sim-mering. Hold 20 minutes.

4. Remove from heat. Cool promptly in cold water.

SOFT COOKED EGGS

COLD WATER METHOD: Follow dire-tions for Hard-Cooked Eggs – Cold Wat-Method. Let stand 2 to 4 minutes, depend-ing on how done you like your eggs. Co-eggs at once in cold water for sever-seconds to prevent further cooking and make them easier to handle.

BOILING WATER METHOD: Follow dire-tions for Hard-Cooked Eggs–Boiling Wat-Method, but after placing eggs in boilir-water, turn off heat, cover, and let star-6 to 8 minutes. Cool as above.

FLUFFY
SCRAMBLED EGGS

6 eggs
½ teaspoon salt
⅛ teaspoon pepper
6 tablespoons milk or light cream
2 tablespoons butter or margarine

Break eggs one at a time into a cup, then turn each into a medium-size bowl.

Add salt, pepper, and milk or cream.

Beat with rotary egg beater until yolks and whites are thoroughly mixed.

Heat butter or margarine in 9-inch skillet until it is hot enough to make a drop of water sizzle.

5. Tilt skillet to cover bottom and sides with melted fat.

6. Reduce heat. Pour in egg mixture. Eggs should cook slowly. Too high a heat will toughen them.

7. Cook slowly, lifting partly cooked and set eggs from the bottom with a spatula or fork. The thin, uncooked part will flow to the bottom. Don't stir constantly.

8. Continue cooking until eggs are thickened throughout but still moist and just a bit underdone. Remember, the heat remaining in the skillet after you take it from the range will finish cooking the eggs. Makes 3 to 4 servings.

THE FRENCH OMELET

there is one recipe, which if mastered, can establish you as a masterful and artful cook. That is the versatile French omelet that can be a main dish for any meal, and with minor changes can be a dessert. When properly done it is tender, delectable. There is a trick and technique to making one and it takes study and practice to learn.

● An omelet, when perfectly done, is soft in the center and firm on the outside. Don't be discouraged if the first few you make are not perfect, for it takes practice to master the technique. It is time worth spending, however, because once you learn the simple tricks you will never forget them. Even before you crack the first egg, there are some things to learn.

● First you should select your skillet. Choose one that is rounded where the bottom and sides meet. It can be made of cast aluminum, stainless steel, or cast iron. For an omelet made with four eggs, a 10-inch skillet is best. Use a 7-inch one for an omelet of two or three eggs. An omelet of four eggs is the largest you should make. Any larger than that becomes difficult to handle and may not be as tender as it should be. Omelets take only minutes to make and you will have greater success if you make small ones, one after another, than if you try making a large one.

● The skillet must be seasoned before you use it because the eggs must be able to move freely in the pan. The pan cannot be sticky. Clean the skillet with a soapy steel-wool pad until it is bright and glistening. Wash and dry it. Pour pure vegetable oil into the skillet until it is one inch deep. Set it over medium heat and heat for 20 minutes. Pour off the oil carefully—you can use it in other cooking. Wipe the skillet with a paper towel. It is now seasoned and ready for your omelet. Some people set aside one skillet and use it for nothing but omelets so they don't have to season the pan again until it begins to stick. If, however, you use this skillet for other cooking, you will have to season it each time you want to use it for an omelet.

● Have everything you are going to need and use ready and at hand. Let the eggs stand at room temperature for an hour before you begin. If you are going to make a filled omelet, make the filling first.

● Now read the recipe and study the illustrations carefully. Be sure you understand it from beginning to end, because once you begin, everything goes quickly—it takes only about 2 minutes from start to finish—and you won't have time to stop and look at the recipes and pictures.

THE OMELET

4 eggs
¼ teaspoon salt
Dash of pepper
1 tablespoon butter or margarine

1. Break the eggs into a bowl. Add the salt and pepper.

2. Beat the eggs briskly with a fork only until the whites and yolks are mixed. Don't beat too much. The mixture should look stringy. When you lift your fork, you'll see the eggs have actually formed a string on it.

3. Put the seasoned skillet over high heat and let it get sizzling hot.

4. Put the butter or margarine into the sizzling skillet. Spear it with a fork and stir it around quickly to coat the bottom and sides of the pan.

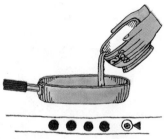

5. The butter must be hot when the eggs are added—the temperature is most important to a successful omelet. It will foam. When the foam subsides, pour in the eggs quickly. If by some mischance the butter turned brown, throw it out, wipe the skillet with a paper towel, and start again.

6. Here you must begin to work quickly. Hold the fork in your right hand and the handle of the skillet in your left. Stir the eggs rapidly in a circular motion with the flat of the fork and, at the same time, shake the pan vigorously over the heat. Stir just until the free liquid begins to set.

7. Pat the omelet with the back of the fork so it lies even in the pan. Let it stand 2 to 3 seconds.

8. Shake the pan. The omelet should move easily and freely. It is now ready for you to roll. If you plan to fill it, the filling would be added now.

9. Take the fork and start rolling the omelet gently. Lift up the side of the omelet nearest the skillet handle and fold a third of the omelet over the center. Use a delicate, light touch to keep the omelet fluffy.

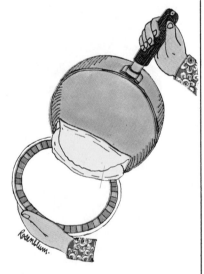

10. Hold a heated serving plate in your left hand. Grasp the pan handle in your right hand, palm up. Tilt the pan over the plate and let the omelet roll out onto it. If you want your omelet to have a shiny top, rub the top with some butter or margarine. Serve at once, for omelets lose their tenderness if they are kept warm to wait. Makes 2 servings.

HOT COCOA

¼ cup cocoa
3 tablespoons sugar
Dash of salt
⅓ cup water
3 cups milk
Marshmallows, peppermint sticks, or whipped cream

1. Mix cocoa, sugar, and salt in a medium size saucepan. Stir in water slowly, blending ingredients to keep smooth.

2. Cook over medium heat, stirring constantly, until mixture comes to boiling. Boil 2 minutes, stirring constantly.

Remove from heat. Stir in milk slowly.

Return to heat. Cook just until bubbles [ap]pear around the edge of mixture. Do [no]t let the cocoa boil.

[Pour] cocoa into cups. Put a marsh-[m]allow or peppermint stick in each cup [or] top each with a spoonful of whipped [cr]eam. Makes 4 servings.

COFFEE

[Ti]ps for Brewing

[BU]Y THE RIGHT GRIND FOR YOUR [CO]FFEE MAKER. Coarse or regular for [pe]rked, filtered, or steeped coffee; fine or [dri]p grind for drip coffee makers and most [va]cuum pots.

[ST]ART WITH A CLEAN POT. The bitter oil [tha]t clings to the inside of the pot can ruin [a] cup of coffee. Scrub the pot with a brush [—d]on't just rinse it—especially around the [sp]out and tube.

USE COLD WATER FRESH FROM THE TAP. Measure the same way every time. You can decide the strength you want, but the Coffee Brewing Institute says to use 2 level measuring tablespoons (a standard coffee measure) for each 6-ounce cup of water.

SERVE COFFEE FRESHLY BREWED. Always remove the grounds as soon as the coffee has completed brewing.

TEA

Use a preheated teapot. This holds the water temperature at a high level during the brewing. Rinse the pot with boiling water. Even for one cup of tea it is best to use a teapot, but if this isn't possible, cover the cup with a saucer during the brewing, thus turning it into a teapot.

Use enough tea. One tea bag or one teaspoon of loose tea per cup is right.

Use freshly drawn water. Bring it to a full rolling boil and pour it over the tea in the teapot.

Time the brewing—3 to 5 minutes. Don't guess. It takes time for the tea leaves to unfold and release their flavor. Some teas brew light, some dark, so color is no indication of strength. Proper timing is the only way to be sure to have a good cup of tea.

Stir tea before pouring into the cups to make sure it is uniformly strong.

If weaker tea is desired, just add a little hot water after it has brewed.

RICE

rice is one of the most convenient and versatile foods we have. It's easy to cook, combines well with innumerable foods, keeps well, is easy to store, and is economical. There is no waste—every ounce is edible. And for a variety of texture and flavor, there are several different kinds of rice to try.

White rice is probably the most familiar and popular variety of rice. It is often called regular rice. The hull, germ, outer bran layers, and most of the inner bran have been removed. It may be either short, medium, or long grain. The short- or medium-grain varieties have short, plump grains which cook tender and moist and tend to cling together. They are good for puddings and other dishes in which a soft consistency is desired. Long-grain rice, slightly higher in price, is four to five times as long as the grain is wide. It cooks light and fluffy and the grains tend to separate from each other in cooking. This type is preferred for serving as a vegetable or for curry and Oriental dishes.

Parboiled rice, also called processed or converted, is white rice that has been partly cooked before milling. Special care is taken to retain the natural vitamins and minerals.

Precooked rice, known to many as instant rice because it needs so little preparation, is milled rice that has been completely cooked and then had the water extracted.

Brown rice is unpolished wholegrain rice that has had only the outer hull removed. It has a nutlike flavor, is richer in vitamins than polished rice, has a shorter shelf life, and takes longer to cook.

Wild rice is not a true rice but the seed of a reedlike water grass native to Minnesota and other Northern states. It is quite expensive because of the short supply and difficult harvesting.

There are also many rice products you can buy. These include the seasoned rices, canned and frozen specialties, and packaged combinations.

How much rice should you cook? You must remember rice swells three to four times its measure as it cooks. Use this chart as a guide for the yield of the different kinds of rice:

1 cup uncooked	Measure after cooking
Regular white rice	3 cups
Parboiled rice	4 cups
Precooked rice	2 to 3 cups
Brown rice	4 cups

FLUFFY RICE

1 cup regular white rice
2 cups water
1 teaspoon salt

1. Measure rice into a 3-quart saucepan that has a tight-fitting lid.

2. Add water and salt.

3. Place over high heat and bring to a full rolling boil. Stir several times during cooking.

4. Lower heat to simmer. Cover pan.

5. Simmer rice 14 minutes. Do not remove cover or stir rice.

6. Uncover the pan. Look to see that the water has been absorbed and test the rice by tasting it to see that it is tender. Simmer a little longer if needed.

1 cup rice
1½ teaspoons salt
2½ cups boiling water

7. Remove from heat. Turn rice into serving dish. Fluff with fork or slotted spoon. Makes 3 cups (4 servings).

OVEN-BAKED RICE

1. Heat oven to 350° F.

2. Put ingredients for Fluffy Rice into a 3-quart baking dish. Cover.

3. Bake 25 to 30 minutes or until rice is tender.

1. Heat oven to 375° F.

2. Spread rice in shallow baking pan.

3. Bake, stirring occasionally, until rice grains are golden brown. Remove pan from oven.

4. Turn oven heat to 400° F.

5. Put toasted rice into 1½-quart casserole with a tight-fitting cover.

6. Stir in salt and boiling water. Cover.

7. Bake 20 minutes. Makes 4 servings. Note: You can toast a quantity of rice at one time then store it in a tightly covered jar for future use.

MAIN DISHES

OVEN-FRIED CHICKEN

2 broiler-fryers
(about 2 pounds each),
cut in pieces
½ cup melted butter or margarine
(¼ pound stick)
½ cup all-purpose flour
1 teaspoon salt
¼ teaspoon pepper
1 teaspoon paprika

1. Heat the oven to 425° F.

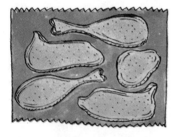

2. Wash chicken pieces. Pat pieces dry with paper towels.

3. Put melted butter or margarine into a 13x9x2-inch pan.

4. Put flour, salt, pepper, and paprika in a paper bag. Close tightly; shake.

5. Put three or four pieces of chicken into the bag. Shake to coat them with flour

mixture. Repeat until all chicken pieces have been coated with flour mixture.

6. Place chicken pieces, skin side down, in single layer in prepared pan.

7. Bake 30 minutes.

8. Turn chicken.

9. Bake 15 minutes or until tender.

CREOLE PORK CHOPS

2 green peppers
2 large onions
2 tablespoons fat or pure vegetable oil
4 loin pork chops (1-inch thick each)
1 can (1 pound) tomatoes
1 envelope Italian-style salad-
dressing mix

1. Cut tops from green peppers. Remove seeds and white membranes. Cut peppers into strips.

2. Peel and slice onions. Separate the slices into rings.

3. Heat fat or oil in large skillet. Add green-pepper strips and onion rings. Sauté 10 minutes. Remove from skillet. Set aside.

4. Add chops to fat or oil remaining in skillet. Cook until brown on bottom. Turn and brown the second side. Remove chops. Pour off fat remaining in pan.

5. Pour tomatoes into skillet. Stir to scrape up all brown bits on bottom of skillet. Stir in salad-dressing mix.

6. Put green peppers, onions, and chops into skillet. Cover. Bring to boiling. Lower heat so liquid bubbles slowly (simmers).

7. Cook 50 to 60 minutes or until chops are tender when pierced with a 2-tine fork. Makes 4 servings.

MACARONI FRANKFURTER CASSEROLE

4 quarts water
1 tablespoon salt
1 package (8 ounces) elbow macaroni
8 frankfurters
1 can (14½ ounces) evaporated milk
½ cup water
1 can (10½ ounces) cream of mushroom
soup, undiluted
½ pound process American cheese,
cubed
2 teaspoons grated Parmesan cheese
1 teaspoon prepared mustard
(the kind from a jar)

1. Put 4 quarts of water and the salt into a large pot. Cover and bring to boiling. Add macaroni. Cook, uncovered, 6 to 7 minutes or until macaroni is just tender. Stir occasionally. The best way to test the macaroni is to take a piece and bite it.

2. While macaroni cooks, turn on the oven to 350° F. Grease a 2-quart casserole.

3. Cut 6 frankfurters into 1-inch pieces. Cut 2 more in half, lengthwise.

4. When macaroni is tender, drain it into a colander. Turn it into the casserole.

5. Combine evaporated milk, water, undiluted mushroom soup, American and Parmesan cheeses, and mustard in a medium-size saucepan. Cook over medium heat, stirring constantly, until cheeses are melted.

6. Pour cheese sauce over macaroni in casserole. Toss with a fork until macaroni is coated. Stir in cut-up frankfurters. Use halved frankfurters on top like the spokes of a wheel. Place in preheated oven.

7. Bake 25 to 30 minutes or until lightly browned. Makes 6 servings.

16

TUNA FLORENTINE

1 package (10 ounces) fresh, washed spinach
½ teaspoon salt
2 cans (7 ounces each) tuna
3 tablespoons butter or margarine
3 tablespoons flour
1 teaspoon salt   2 cups milk
⅛ teaspoon pepper
¼ cup grated Parmesan cheese
2 tablespoons melted butter or margarine
Lemon wedges

Rinse spinach. Put in large saucepan. Add ½ teaspoon salt. Spinach, because it contains so much water, should cook in just the water that clings to the leaves.

Cover pan. Cook over medium heat, stirring occasionally, 5 to 10 minutes or until tender. Drain very well, pressing out all the water possible. Set aside.

Drain oil from tuna. Separate tuna into flakes. Set aside.

4. Melt butter or margarine in medium-size saucepan. Remove from heat. Blend in flour, salt, and pepper.

5. Stir in milk gradually, blending to keep smooth. Cook over medium heat, stirring constantly, until sauce comes to boiling. Boil 1 minute. Turn off heat.

6. Add Parmesan. Stir until it melts.

7. Preheat broiler.

8. Divide spinach among 4 individual ramekins or baking dishes. Top with flaked tuna.

9. Pour sauce over tuna in each dish. Drizzle with melted butter or margarine.

10. Put dishes on a cookie sheet. Slip under broiler. Broil 5 minutes or until sauce bubbles. Serve with lemon wedges. Makes 4 servings.

SPAGHETTI AND MEATBALLS

Did you know that spaghetti is only one of many hundreds of different types and shapes of dried dough that the Italians call *pasta*? Macaroni is used by many to describe the whole family, though pasta is becoming more familiar to us every day.

There are many legends as to the origin of pasta. But, whether you believe that Marco Polo brought it to Italy from China or discount the rumor because mention of macaroni can be found in a book published more than 500 years before he was born—you know it is a food you can enjoy in innumerable ways. Someone has said there are enough shapes and ways of serving pasta that you could serve it every day in the year and never repeat yourself.

To enjoy pasta properly, you should learn to cook it correctly. First, the pasta should be fresh. It can lose flavor if kept on the shelf too long. And, it should be cooked just before serving. You will need a very large pot—one about 8 quarts—since pasta requires a large amount of water. The recommended proportions: 3 quarts of water for 8 ounces of pasta.

How much should you cook? This can depend on the appetites of those you're cooking for, but generally, ½ to 1 cup of cooked pasta is allowed per person. To figure out how much you'll need, remember 1 cup (4 ounces) of uncooked pasta equals 2 cups cooked.

Always start with cold water. Add a tablespoon of salt for each 3 quarts of water and bring to a rapid boil. This means that the surface of the water should be moving vigorously and steadily. You can add a tablespoon of olive oil, if you like, to keep the pasta from sticking.

Add the pasta. If it is long strands of spaghetti, don't break them. Hold a bunch of spaghetti near the end and lower it gently into the boiling water.

It will soften as it enters the water and you can push the rest down gently. Leave the pot uncovered and boil the spaghetti rapidly. Stir occasionally with a large wooden spoon so all pieces will be cooked to the same doneness. Stir gently—don't break the pieces.

How long to cook it? Pasta should never be soft and mushy—then it is overcooked. Italians, who should know, say spaghetti should be cooked al dente. This translates literally as "to the tooth," which means the pasta is cooked until it bites firmly but chewy. Check the directions on the package.

Then 3 to 4 minutes before the sug-

18

gested time, start testing. Take a strand and bite it. Test every minute until it meets the test of al dente. The total cooking time will vary with the type of pasta (the thinner the spaghetti, the less cooking time) and your own taste of how you like it.

Remove the pot from the heat and turn the spaghetti into a colander you have previously placed in the sink. Let it drain but don't rinse it. That will make it cold.

Pasta can be served with just butter and cheese, but it also lends itself to a variety of sauces. There are many excellent ones you can buy in cans, jars, and packages, but there is great satisfaction in making your own. Let's do a classic one—tomato sauce with meatballs. The sauce will freeze well so you can make it anytime and have it on hand to heat and serve.

MARINARA SAUCE WITH MEATBALLS

MEATBALLS
1 pound ground chuck
1 cup soft bread crumbs
2 tablespoons chopped parsley
1 egg
2 tablespoons grated Parmesan cheese
2 teaspoons grated onion
½ teaspoon salt
¼ teaspoon pepper
¼ cup olive or pure vegetable oil

1. Combine chuck, bread crumbs, parsley, egg, cheese, grated onion, salt, and pepper in large bowl. Mix thoroughly but lightly.

2. Shape into small meatballs about 1½ inches in diameter.

3. Heat oil in skillet. Brown meatballs on all sides. Put only as many into the

skillet as will fit. Turn meatballs carefully with a wooden spoon. Try not to pierce them to avoid losing any of the juices from the meat.

4. Remove meatballs from skillet as they brown and set aside.

5. Make the sauce: Heat 3 T. vegetable oil in large saucepan. Add ¾ c. chopped onion and 1 clove garlic (crushed).

6. Cook 10 minutes.

7. Add 2 cans (1 lb., 1 oz.) Italian plum tomatoes, 2 cans (6 oz.) tomato paste, 1 c. water, 1 t. salt, 1 T. sugar, 2 t. leaf oregano (crumbled), ½ t. leaf basil (crumbled), and ⅛ t. dried red pepper flakes. Mix thoroughly.

8. Cover pan. Bring sauce to boiling. Reduce heat. Simmer sauce gently 1½ hours, stirring occasionally.

9. Uncover. Add meatballs. Simmer 30 minutes or until sauce is as thick as desired.

10. Serve over your cooked, hot spaghetti. Pass grated Parmesan cheese to sprinkle over each serving.

How to eat spaghetti? Spear a few strands on a fork and twirl it round and round on the plate or a spoon.

STUFFED EGGS AU GRATIN

8 eggs
½ teaspoon onion salt
½ teaspoon Worcestershire sauce
1 can (2¼ ounces) deviled ham
2 tablespoons mayonnaise or salad dressing
1 package (10 ounces) frozen French-style green beans
1 can (10½ ounces) condensed cream of celery soup
⅔ cup milk
1 package (8 ounces) shredded process American cheese

1. Put eggs in saucepan. Add enough lukewarm water to cover tops of eggs.

2. Heat quickly until water boils.

3. Remove saucepan from heat. Cover. Let stand 15 minutes.

4. Pour off hot water. Add cold water to saucepan immediately.

5. To crack egg, tap entire surface of shell on work surface. Roll between palms of hands to loosen shell. Peel shell from egg. Repeat with rest of eggs.

. Cut eggs in half lengthwise. Remove
olks and put them in a small bowl.

. Mash yolks in bowl. Mix in onion salt,
Worcestershire, deviled ham, and may-
nnaise or salad dressing. Fill cavities
 egg whites with yolk mixture.

3. Cook beans as directed on package.
Drain. Place in 8x8x2-inch baking dish.

9. Arrange stuffed eggs on beans.

0. Mix soup, milk, and half the cheese.
Pour into baking dish around the eggs.

1. Sprinkle top of casserole with remaining shredded cheese.

2. Cover with transparent plastic wrap
r aluminum foil. Chill until ready to bake.

3. Remove from refrigerator and let
tand at room temperature 30 minutes.

14. Uncover. Bake at 350° F. for 30
minutes. Makes 4 servings.

MEATBALL PIZZA

t's fun to bake with yeast
and it's really easy. Once
you learn the hows and
whys you can turn your
skills to making wonder-
ful breads and rolls and
delicious coffee cakes and
buns and the beautiful
holiday cakes and breads.

Let's start with a fun recipe—pizza with a
meatball topping.

Before you begin you should know
something about yeast. Yeast is a living
plant that, under proper conditions,

21

grows and multiplies to make the dough rise. It is available in two forms, active dry and compressed. The active dry yeast comes in individual packets and can be stored on the shelf. Compressed yeast comes in cakes, is perishable, and must be kept in the refrigerator.

Yeast needs warmth to do its job, and temperature is most important in all steps.

Dissolving the yeast: The water in which yeast is dissolved should be warm but not hot. Rinse a bowl and measuring cup with hot water before you begin, to help maintain temperature. Then measure the warm water into the bowl. Check the temperature with a thermometer—it should read between 105° and 115° F.— or test it by dropping a few drops on the inside of your wrist. It should feel comfortably warm but not hot.

Rising of the dough: After the dough is mixed and kneaded it is set aside to rise. As it rises, the action of the yeast changes the firm, heavy ball of dough into a big, light, puffy one. It must be kept evenly warm and away from drafts to work properly. The best temperature is 85° F. An easy way to keep the dough warm is to set it over hot water. Fill a

large bowl two-thirds full of hot water, place a wire cake rack over the bowl, and set the bowl of dough on the rack. Cover completely with a towel and check the water from time to time to be sure it is still hot.

PIZZA DOUGH

1 cup warm water (105° to 115° F.)
1 packet active dry yeast or
1 cake compressed yeast
1 teaspoon salt
2 tablespoons pure vegetable oil or olive oil
3 cups sifted all-purpose flour (about)

1. Measure warm water into mixing bowl

2. Sprinkle in dry yeast or crumble in compressed yeast. Stir until dissolved.

3. Add and stir in salt and oil.

4. Add 2 cups flour. Beat smooth. Mix in enough more flour until dough cleans side of bowl and doesn't stick to your fingers

5. Sprinkle board lightly with flour. Turn dough out onto board.

Dust hands lightly with flour. Press ⸺ugh out flat. Pick up edge farthest from ⸺u with the fingers of both hands and ⸺ld it over on top of edge nearest you. ⸺rinkle board with flour, as you need it, ⸺ keep the dough from sticking.

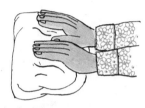

Push dough away from you with the ⸺els of your hands, using a rocking mo-⸺n. Press dough lightly as you push. ⸺rn dough a quarter turn around on ⸺ard. Repeat folding, pushing, and turn-⸺g until dough looks full and rounded, ⸺ooth and elastic. You'll see tiny bubbles ⸺st under the surface.

Put dough into greased bowl. Turn ⸺ugh over to bring greased side on top. ⸺is greases the top so it will stay soft

⸺d stretch easily as the dough rises.
Cover bowl with a clean towel. Let ⸺ugh rise in a warm place (85° F.), free ⸺m draft, about 1 hour or until doubled ⸺ bulk.

10. To test for double in bulk: Press the tips of two fingers quickly and lightly about ½ inch into dough. If the indentation remains, the dough is double. If the dent fills in at once, let the dough rise 10 to 15 minutes longer and retest.
11. While dough rises, prepare Meatball Topping. Here's what you'll need:

PIZZA TOPPING

1 pound ground chuck
½ cup packaged bread crumbs
½ teaspoon salt
¼ teaspoon pepper
⅓ cup milk
⅓ cup pure vegetable oil
½ cup chopped onion (1 medium)
1 clove of garlic, crushed
1 can (1 pound, 1 ounce) Italian plum tomatoes
1 can (6 ounces) tomato paste
2 teaspoons leaf oregano, crumbled
½ teaspoon leaf basil, crumbled
1½ teaspoons salt
⅛ teaspoon dried red pepper flakes
2 packages (8 ounces each) mozzarella cheese, sliced

12. Mix ground chuck, bread crumbs, ½ teaspoon salt, pepper, and milk. Shape into 36 small meatballs.
13. Heat oil in large skillet. Add meatballs. Brown on all sides. Remove from skillet and reserve.

14. Add onion and garlic to oil remaining in skillet. Sauté just until soft. Add tomatoes, tomato paste, oregano, basil, 1½ teaspoons salt, and pepper flakes. Cover; bring to boiling. Reduce heat.

15. Simmer sauce 40 minutes. Add meatballs. Simmer 20 minutes longer.

16. Heat oven to 425° F. Grease 2 large cookie sheets.

17. When dough is doubled in bulk, punch it down. Push your fist into the center. Pull edges of dough from sides of bowl to the center. Turn dough over.

18. Turn dough out on lightly floured board. Knead it a few times to distribute the air bubbles. Cut dough in half.

19. Roll out each half on greased cookie sheet to a 13-inch circle. Pinch up edge of each to form a rim.

20. Spoon half the sauce over each circle, spread to rim. Top with cheese slices.

21. Bake about 25 minutes or until rim of crust is golden and cheese melts. Cut in wedges to serve.

ROAST STUFFED TURKEY

Roasting a turkey to golden perfection is a simple technique. Making smooth gravy is easy as 1-2-3.

Ready-to-cook turkeys are sold fresh and frozen (most are frozen). They are trimmed and fully drawn and have the giblets neatly packaged inside the breast cavity. You can buy them in sizes from 4 to 24 pounds and larger. Some turkeys come with very special cooking directions. They should be followed exactly.

When buying turkey under 12 pounds, allow ¾ to 1 pound per serving. For birds over 12 pounds, allow ½ to ¾ pound per serving. Remember, that is per serving, not per person. You'll want to have second helpings.

If you're buying a frozen turkey, allow enough time for it to thaw completely. Put the bird, in its original wrapping, on a tray and place it in the refrigerator. It takes 1 to 3 days. Or, place the wrapped bird in a large pan and let the turkey thaw overnight at room temperature.

COOKING THE GIBLETS

Do this a day ahead and refrigerate.
Ready-to-cook turkey, thawed
1 onion, sliced
Handful of celery tops
1 teaspoon salt
4 peppercorns
Water

1. Wash and dry giblets and neck. Put all but liver in saucepan.

2. Add onion, celery tops, salt, peppercorns, and water to cover. Cover, bring to boiling; reduce heat. Simmer 2 hours or until gizzard is tender. Add liver during last 20 minutes.

3. Strain. Reserve broth.

4. Remove meat from neck. Chop neck meat and giblets. Reserve.

1. Cube bread or tear it into large crumbs. Pile it lightly in cup to measure it. You should have 4 quarts.

2. Put bread in large, shallow pan. Toast lightly in 325° F. oven.

3. Melt ½ cup butter or margarine in skillet. Add onions and celery. Cook until soft but not brown. Add 1 cup butter or margarine. Heat until melted.

4. Put bread cubes, salt, sage, and parsley in large bowl. Add onion-celery mixture and turkey broth. Mix well.

SAGE BREAD STUFFING

This amount of stuffing is enough for a 16- to 18-pound turkey. You can adjust it to the size of your bird. Allow 1 cup bread cubes for each pound ready-to-cook weight. Two regular slices of bread give 1 cup of cubes.

32 slices bread (about)
½ cup butter or margarine
2 cups chopped onions (2 large)
1½ cups chopped celery
1 cup butter or margarine
1 teaspoon salt
1 tablespoon leaf sage, crumbled
2 tablespoons chopped parsley
½ cup turkey broth

ROASTING THE TURKEY

Plan to start roasting turkey so it will be done about 30 minutes ahead of the time set for dinner. This avoids delay should cooking take longer than estimated. And it allows time for the meat to stand and absorb juices so bird is easier to carve.

1. Heat oven to 325° F.

2. Rinse turkey inside and out with cold water. Drain. Pat dry.

3. Spoon stuffing loosely into nèck (wishbone) cavity. Pull neck skin up and over cavity. Skewer to back.

4. Fold wings. Bring wing tips behind shoulder joints.

5. Spoon stuffing lightly into body cavity. Do not pack because stuffing tends to expand during roasting.

6. Push ends of legs under band of skin above the tail. Or, tie a piece of string securely around the tail and tie ends of legs to same string.

7. Place turkey, breast side up, on rack in shallow, open roasting pan. Brush with soft butter or margarine.

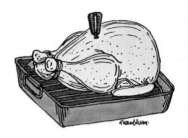

8. Insert meat thermometer so the point is in center of the stuffing.

9. Roast turkey, using time below as guide, until thermometer registers 165° F. Baste turkey, particularly any dry places, occasionally with pan drippings or butter or margarine.

WEIGHT (pounds)	APPROXIMATE HOURS
6 to 12	2 to 2½
8 to 12	2½ to 3
12 to 16	3 to 3¾
16 to 20	3¾ to 4½
20 to 24	4½ to 5½

10. Remove turkey to heated platter. Keep warm. Let turkey rest at least 20 minutes before carving.

TURKEY GRAVY

1. Pour fat and meat juices from roasting pan into a bowl. Be sure to leave all brown bits in the pan. These contain the "essence" that will give flavor and color to your gravy.

2. Let fat rise to top of juices. Skim off fat and put in a second bowl.

3. For each cup of gravy you want, measure 1 tablespoon fat into the roasting pan. Set over low heat.

Measure 1 tablespoon flour for each [cu]p of gravy. Blend into fat in pan. [Co]ok until bubbly, stirring constantly. [Br]own it slightly if more color and [fla]vor are desired.

You will need a cup of liquid for [ea]ch cup of finished gravy. Use the [re]served meat juices and turkey broth. [If] you need more liquid, you can use [wa]ter. Add the cool or lukewarm [liq]uid to flour-fat mixture all at once.

[C]ook, stirring constantly, until thick[en]ed, scraping up all brown bits from [pa]n and blending them into gravy.

[Add] giblets. Simmer gently 5 min[ut]es. Taste gravy. Season, if needed, [wi]th salt and pepper.

OLD-FASHIONED MEAT LOAF

4 slices fresh white bread
2 eggs
2 pounds ground chuck
1 cup very finely chopped onion
[1] cup very finely chopped green pepper
2 teaspoons salt
½ teaspoon garlic salt
¼ teaspoon celery salt
½ teaspoon dry mustard
¼ teaspoon pepper
1 tablespoon Worcestershire sauce
¼ cup milk
¾ cup catsup

1. Turn on oven and heat to 400° F.

2. Tear bread into crumbs with fingers. (Or make crumbs in a blender: Tear one slice of bread into large pieces and put in the blender container. Cover and whirl just until bread is crumbed. Empty crumbs onto a piece of wax paper. Crumb the remaining slices, one at a time.) You should have 2 cups of crumbs.

3. Beat eggs slightly in a large bowl.

4. Mix the chuck into the eggs lightly. Then mix in bread crumbs, onion, and green pepper. Always mix ground beef lightly to keep it tender and juicy.

5. Add the salt, garlic salt, celery salt, mustard, pepper, Worcestershire, milk, and ¼ cup of catsup. Mix lightly until all ingredients are well combined.

6. Turn the meat mixture from the bowl into a shallow baking pan. Moisten hands and pat the meat into a loaf shape.

7. With the side of your hand, or the handle of a wooden spoon, make 2 indentations the length of the loaf. Spread the remaining catsup in the indentations.

8. Bake 50 minutes.

9. Transfer loaf from pan to a heated platter with two large spatulas. Spoon some of the juices from the pan over the loaf. Makes 8 servings.

SALADS

CHICKEN CRANBERRY SALAD

a beautiful molded salad makes a perfect summer meal. Gelatin is one of the easiest things to prepare though there are some secrets you should know and follow that will lead to success.

■ To have an evenly set mold, the gelatin must be completely dissolved in boiling water or other liquid before any additions are made.

■ When you add fruits, vegetables, meat or fish to gelatin, you want them to be distributed evenly throughout the mixture. You don't want them to sink to the bottom or float to the top. To achieve this, let the gelatin set until syrupy—about the consistency of honey—before folding in the other ingredients.

■ To make a gelatin mold of two or more layers, chill each layer just until set before adding the next one. Touch the top of the layer with your fingertip. It should be set but sticky. The next layer needs this "stickiness" to make it cling to the first layer as it chills. If the first layer is too firm, the layers may slide apart when you unmold them. The gelatin mixture for the second layer (or succeeding layers) should be cool and slightly thickened before you turn it into the mold. If it is warm, it could soften the layer beneath and cause the two mixtures to mix.

■ Unmolding gelatin can take a bit of practice. You can see exactly how it is done in the how-to pictures at the end of the recipe below. Before you start to unmold gelatin, be sure it is completely firm. The top should be smooth, not at all sticky, and the gelatin should not sag if you tilt the mold.

FIRST LAYER

1 package (3 ounces)
lemon-flavored gelatin
1 cup boiling water
½ cup cold water
1 can (1 pound) whole
cranberry sauce
¾ cup chopped, blanched almonds

SECOND LAYER

1 package (3 ounces)
lemon-flavored gelatin
1 cup boiling water
½ cup cold water
1 tablespoon minced onion
½ cup mayonnaise or salad dressing
1 teaspoon salt
¼ teaspoon pepper
½ cup diced celery
2 tablespoons chopped green pepper
2 cups diced, cooked chicken
Crisp salad greens

MAKE FIRST LAYER

1. Empty contents of 1 package of gelatin into medium-size bowl.

2. Add 1 cup boiling water. Stir until all gelatin is dissolved. Stir in ½ cup cold water.

3. Chill until mixture is slightly thickened. It should be about the consistency of honey.

4. Fold in cranberry sauce and almonds.

5. Pour into 2-quart mold. Chill until set but not firm.

MAKE SECOND LAYER

6. Dissolve second package of gelatin and add cold water as you did to the first package (see step 2).

7. Combine onion, mayonnaise or salad dressing, salt, and pepper. Add to gelatin mixture. Mix well.

8. Chill mixture in bowl just until it begins to set.

9. Fold in celery, green pepper, and chicken.

10. Turn into mold on top of cranberry layer.

11. Chill several hours or overnight until salad is firm. When ready to serve, unmold onto serving plate:

12. Dip a small, pointed knife in warm water and run tip between gelatin and mold to loosen gelatin.

13. Moisten top of gelatin. Moisten a chilled plate. Moistening the surfaces will make it easy to move the gelatin to the center of the plate after unmolding.

15. Lift mold from water. Hold upright and shake gently to loosen gelatin from mold. If gelatin doesn't loosen, repeat step 14.

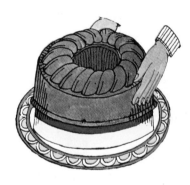

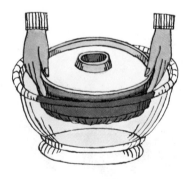

14. Dip mold into warm water. Be sure water is not hot or gelatin will melt; work quickly. Dip mold just up to the rim and remove quickly. Don't keep it in the water more than 10 seconds.

16. Place inverted plate on top of mold. Hold plate and mold firmly and turn them over. Set on table. Lift mold gently.

17. Center salad on plate. Garnish with crisp salad greens and tomato wedges, if desired. Makes 6 to 8 servings.

TOSSED CHEESE-CRACKER SALAD

½ teaspoon dry mustard
½ teaspoon sugar
½ teaspoon salt
¼ teaspoon garlic powder
½ cup wine vinegar
⅔ cup pure vegetable oil
1 medium-size head Boston lettuce
½ medium-size head curly endive
8 green onions
1 medium-size cucumber
2 firm, ripe tomatoes
½ cup coarsely broken cheese crackers

1. Combine mustard, sugar, salt, garlic powder, vinegar, and oil in screw-top jar. Cover securely. Shake well. Refrigerate while making salad.

2. Remove bruised leaves from lettuce. Cut out core with sharp paring knife. Hold under cold, running water to separate leaves. Shake off excess water. Pat dry. Refrigerate in paper-towel-lined vegetable crisper or in a plastic bag in crisper.

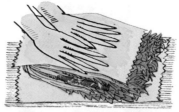

3. Wash the curly endive well in several changes of water. Shake off excess. Dry and store as you did the lettuce.

4. Remove root ends from onions; peel. Slice thinly.

5. Cut ends from cucumbers. Run tines of fork down length of cucumber. Repeat all the way around. Slice thinly.

6. Core tomatoes. Cut in thin wedges.

7. Tear lettuce and endive into bite-size pieces. Put in salad bowl. Add onions, cucumber, and tomatoes. Pour on dressing. Toss with salad fork and spoon until coated. Sprinkle with crackers.

CAKES

BUTTER CAKES

BUSY-DAY CAKE

2¼ cups sifted cake flour
3 teaspoons double-action baking powder
1 teaspoon salt
½ cup shortening
1½ cups sugar
2 eggs
1 cup milk
1½ teaspoons vanilla

There are two types of cakes: butter cakes and foam cakes. Butter-type cakes are those made with shortening—butter, margarine, or vegetable shortening. Foam-type cakes include angel food and sponge cakes that contain no shortening and chiffon cakes that are made with oil. We are going to make a butter-type cake. Before you start to make your cake:

1. Read the recipe carefully all the way through and be sure you understand it.

2. Assemble all the ingredients. They should be at room temperature before you begin to mix the cake, so let them stand on the kitchen counter for a while.

3. Get together all your utensils.

4. Place the oven rack in the center of the oven. Heat the oven to 350° F.

5. Grease two 9x1½-inch layer-cake pans. Use a pastry brush or a piece of wax paper and spread about 1½ teaspoons of vegetable shortening evenly over the bottom and sides of each pan. Sprinkle each pan with 1½ teaspoons of flour. Shake or rotate the pan to coat it with flour. Turn the pan upside down and shake out any excess.

1. Sift some flour onto a piece of wax paper. We sift before we measure to be sure of getting accurate measurements because flour packs down as it stands in the box. Set the empty sifter on a second piece of wax paper.

2. Spoon the sifted flour into a measuring cup. Do it lightly. Don't tap or shake the cup or the flour will pack down and your sifting will be wasted. Put enough flour into the cup so it heaps up slightly.

3. Bring the edge of the spatula all the way across the top of the cup to level the flour. Put the flour into the empty sifter. Measure the second cup and a quarter cup and put them into the sifter.

4. Measure the baking powder and salt, leveling them as you did the flour. Add them to the sifter. Sift the three ingredients onto the piece of wax paper.

Pack the shortening into a half-cup measure. Level it as you did the flour with the edge of the spatula. Measure and level the sugar.

Put the shortening, sugar, and the eggs into the large bowl of the electric mixer. Beat at high speed for 3 minutes. Turn off the mixer.

Measure milk. Add vanilla to milk.

Take your spatula and divide the flour mixture into four parts.

Add one fourth the flour mixture to the shortening mixture. Beat at low speed on mixer until just blended. Do not overmix. Overmixing once you start to add the flour can make your cake tough and dry.

Add one third of the milk mixture. Beat at low speed until blended. Stop the mixer once in awhile and scrape batter from sides of bowl with a rubber scraper.

Repeat steps 9 and 10 until all the ingredients are used. Your last addition will be flour.

Pour the batter into the greased and floured cake pans, dividing it evenly.

13. Place the pans on the oven rack. Put one in each corner and have them about an inch from the sides of the oven.

14. Bake layers 30 to 35 minutes. To test to see whether they are done, touch the center of the layer quickly and lightly with your fingertip. If no mark remains on the cake it is done.

15. Remove the layers from the oven, using a pot holder, and place them on wire cake racks. Let them stand for 10 minutes.

16. Loosen layers around the sides of the pans with a spatula or thin-bladed knife. Shake gently to free cake from pans.

17. Turn upside down on second wire rack or flat plate. Remove pan. Quickly turn right side up on rack. Cool cake completely.

FOAM CAKES

The cakes we call foam cakes—sponge, angel food and chiffon—are leavened by the air you beat into eggs. They are not difficult to make. Let's make a sponge cake as cupcakes.

There are many variations of sponge cake. Some are made with egg yolks and whites, some with just egg yolks. Some recipes have no liquid, some call for hot water, some cold water, some hot milk. The main leavener in all sponge cakes is air and a true sponge cake contains no baking powder, though you will find recipes that use it as a help for the heavy egg yolks.

Eggs are the chief ingredient in foam cakes, and the way you handle them is most important to the success of your cake. About an hour before you are going to start making your cake, take the eggs from the refrigerator and separate them. They separate easiest when cold. Let them stand at room temperature an hour. They beat up faster and to greater volume when warm.

One of the most important techniques to learn is how to combine the beaten egg whites with the other ingredients without losing the air you've beaten into them. The air you incorporate into the egg whites expands as the cake bakes and gives you a delicate, light cake. If you lose the air, your cake turns out heavy and compact. To do it properly use the technique known as folding:

1. Pour the egg-yolk mixture onto the beaten egg whites.

2. Take your rubber spatula and gently cut down through the mixture on the side of the bowl away from you.

3. Bring the spatula across the bottom of the bowl.

4. Move the spatula up the side of the bowl nearest you and across the top, bringing some up from the bottom.

5. Turn the bowl one quarter way around. Repeat folding mixture and rotating bowl until the two mixtures are completely combined.

SPONGE CUPCAKES

6 eggs
1 cup sugar
1/4 teaspoon cream of tartar
1 teaspoon grated lemon rind
1 tablespoon lemon juice
1 cup sifted cake flour
1/4 teaspoon salt

1. Separate eggs. Have a large bowl for the egg whites, a smaller bowl for the yolks, and a custard cup. Crack the shell right in the middle by giving the egg a quick, sharp tap on the edge of the custard cup. Press the tips of your thumbs into the crack and pull the halves of the shell apart gently. Keep the yolk in one half and let the white dribble into the custard cup. Then, with a juggling motion, rock the yolk from one shell half to the other to let the rest of the white dribble off. Put the yolk into the smaller bowl and put the white into the large bowl. Repeat with the other 5 eggs. Let them stand at room temperature about 1 hour.

2. Set paper cupcake liners in muffin-pan cups.

3. Heat oven to 350° F.

4. Measure 1/2 cup sugar.

5. Beat the egg whites and cream of tartar until they are foamy.

6. Sprinkle 2 tablespoons sugar onto the egg whites. Beat until the sugar is dissolved. Repeat until you have beaten in 1/2 cup sugar (8 tablespoons). Continue beating until meringue stands in stiff, glossy peaks.

7. Beat egg yolks, the second 1/2 cup sugar, lemon rind, and lemon juice until thick and light.

8. Combine flour and salt. Fold into egg-yolk mixture.

9. Pour egg-yolk mixture onto meringue. Fold yolk mixture into meringue *gently* with rubber spatula until they are thoroughly blended and there are no streaks of whites or yolks.

10. Spoon into prepared muffin-pan cups, filling each one two-thirds full.

11. Bake 12 to 15 minutes or until cake springs back when lightly touched with fingertip.

12. Remove from oven. Cool slightly. Remove from pan but leave in paper cups. Cool completely before frosting.

EASTER LAMB CAKE

1 package white or yellow cake mix
2 packages fluffy white frosting mix
1 raisin or currant
Candied cherry
1 large marshmallow
1½ cups shredded coconut
Tiny, colored gumdrops

1. Grease two 9-inch layer-cake pans. Dust with flour until well coated. Shake out excess flour.

2. Heat oven to 350° F.

3. Prepare cake mix, following directions on package. Pour batter into prepared pans, dividing it evenly.

4. Bake 25 to 30 minutes or until top of cake springs back when lightly touched with fingertip. Remove from oven. Place on wire cake racks.

5. Let cakes stand in pans 10 minutes. To remove them from pans, shake pan gently, using pot holders to check that cake is loose in pan. Put an inverted wire cake rack or large dinner plate on the cake. Grasp cake pan and top rack or plate firmly with both hands. Turn upside down. Cake should drop out.

6. Lift the cake pan from the cake. Put cake rack back on cake and turn over again. Remove top cake rack or dinner plate. Cool cake completely.

7. While cake cools, prepare frosting mix according to package directions.

8. To make the body, cut one layer in half. Place one half, top down on platter. Spread thinly with frosting. Place second half, bottom side down on frosting.

9. To make head, cut second layer in half. Turn bottom up. Measure 4½ inches along cut edge. Cut in 1½ inches.

10. Make a 2-inch-long cut straight up from end of first cut.

1. From end of second cut, cut straight ut to curve of cake.

2. Cut a second piece like this from ther half of layer. Put 2 pieces together ith frosting between.

3. Frost straight-cut edge (the neck) of mb's head. Place close against left side f body.

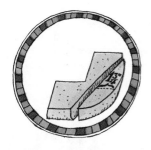

4. From one of the remaining pieces of ake measure 1¾ inches from curved ide. Cut straight across.

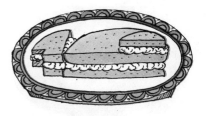

15. Frost one side and place at right of body. This is the lamb's folded leg. Make sure cut sides of all pieces are evenly lined up.

16. Frost entire cake generously, using a spatula to round out corners for the shape of the lamb.

17. Place raisin or currant for eye and a slice of cherry for mouth.

18. Flatten marshmallow with your hand or with a rolling pin. Shape it into oval for an ear. Insert a wooden pick in one end. Push other end of wooden pick into the back of the lamb's head.

19. Sprinkle entire lamb generously with coconut. Arrange gumdrops around neck to form a garland.

MINIATURE FRUITCAKES

3 cups sifted all-purpose flour
1 teaspoon baking powder
1 teaspoon salt
1 teaspoon ground cinnamon
1 cup golden raisins
1 jar (4 ounces) candied red
cherries, quartered
1 jar (4 ounces) candied green
cherries, quartered
1 jar (4 ounces) candied citron
1 jar (4 ounces) candied lemon peel
2 cups slivered, toasted almonds
1 tablespoon grated orange rind
¾ cup orange juice
½ cup currant jelly
1 cup shortening, butter, or margarine
1½ cups sugar
4 eggs
Whole candied cherries
Whole blanched almonds
¼ cup light corn syrup
2 tablespoons water

1. Heat oven to 300° F.

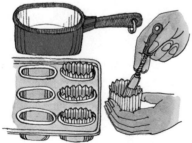

2. Brush about 3 dozen 2½-inch paper baking cups with melted shortening. Set in muffin-pan cups.

3. Sift flour, baking powder, salt, and cinnamon together.

4. Combine raisins, red and green cherries, citron, lemon peel, and almonds; reserve.

5. Beat orange rind and juice and jelly in small bowl; reserve.

6. Beat shortening, sugar, and eggs in large bowl until fluffy.

7. Add flour mixture alternately with orange mixture, beginning and ending with flour.

8. Stir in reserved fruit-nut mixture.

9. Spoon into prepared baking cups, filling two-thirds full.

10. Decorate tops with whole candied cherries or whole almonds.

11. Put a shallow pan on bottom oven rack. Pour in 1 inch of water.

12. Place muffin pans on center rack of oven. Bake cakes 40 to 45 minutes or until cake tester inserted in center comes out clean.

13. Remove from pan. Cool completely on wire racks.

14. Combine corn syrup and water in small saucepan. Bring to boiling. Boil 1 minute. Remove from heat. Cool to lukewarm. Brush over cakes.

FROSTING AND TOPPINGS

4 squares unsweetened chocolate
½ cup butter or margarine
1 package (1 pound) confectioners' sugar
½ cup milk
1 teaspoon vanilla

1. Have about an inch of simmering water in the bottom of a double boiler. Put chocolate and butter or margarine in the top of the double boiler. Set over the water and heat until the chocolate is melted. Remove from heat.

2. Sift the confectioners' sugar into a medium-size bowl.

3. Stir milk and vanilla into the confectioners' sugar.

4. Add the chocolate mixture. Beat until frosting becomes thick enough to spread.

5. Brush crumbs off cake layers gently. Place one layer upside down on a cake plate. Spread about one third of the frosting on top almost to the edge.

6. Place second layer, right side up, on frosting. With the two flat sides of the layers together, the cake will be even.

7. Spread a thin layer of frosting over top and sides of filled cake. This forms a firm base for the rest of the frosting and traps any crumbs that might pull off and spoil the frosting.

LEMON FLUFF FROSTING

1 package (1 pound)
confectioners' sugar
1 package (3 ounces) cream cheese
2 tablespoons milk
½ cup soft butter or margarine
2 teaspoons grated lemon rind
1 tablespoon lemon juice
1 teaspoon vanilla

1. Sift confectioners' sugar.

2. Beat cream cheese, milk, and butter or margarine until light and fluffy.

3. Beat in confectioners' sugar, a cup at a time.

4. Beat in lemon rind, lemon juice, and vanilla.

5. Spread frosting on cupcakes with small spatula.

8. Spread frosting with a broad spatula around sides of cake. Work quickly and bring frosting up to the top of cake to form a rim. This gives a "squaring off" so it won't look sloped.

9. Pile remaining frosting on top of cake. Spread out to meet the rim, using sweeping strokes making swirls.

2. Add boiling water, a small amount a a time, stirring constantly to keep mix ture smooth.

3. Cook over medium heat, stirring cor stantly with wooden spoon, until mixtur thickens and becomes clear. Cook 3 min utes longer.

4. Remove from heat. Stir in butte or margarine and vanilla. Serve warm Makes about 1½ cups.

VANILLA SAUCE

⅓ cup sugar
1½ tablespoons cornstarch
¼ teaspoon salt
1⅔ cups boiling water
3 tablespoons butter or margarine
2 teaspoons vanilla

1. Mix sugar, cornstarch, and salt in medium-size saucepan.

PIES

STRAWBERRY VELVET PIE

1 cup sifted all-purpose flour
½ teaspoon salt
⅓ cup shortening
3 tablespoons cold water
2 packages (3 ounces each) strawberry gelatin
1¾ cups boiling water
1 package (10 ounces) frozen strawberries, thawed
1 package (2 ounces) dessert-topping mix
Cold milk

Heat oven to 425° F.

Sift flour and salt into bowl.

Add shortening. Cut in with pastry ender until shortening is in small parles and mixture resembles cornmeal.

Sprinkle a small amount of cold ater on flour mixture. Blend with a k, using a tossing motion. Repeat til all flour is moistened. Be sure to d the water only a little at a time.

5. Gather dough together so it cleans the bowl. Press firmly into a ball.

6. Sprinkle a small amount of flour onto board. Place ball of dough on board. Flatten slightly with your hand.

7. Rub a small amount of flour over rolling pin. Hold rolling pin *lightly* and place on center of pastry. Roll from center to edge with *quick, light* strokes, lifting rolling pin as you get near the edge. This keeps edges from getting too thin. Don't roll across pastry from edge to edge— keep stroking lightly from center out to edge all around ball of pastry.

8. Be sure pastry is free moving at all times. If it sticks, slide a spatula underneath, lift pastry carefully, and sprinkle board lightly with flour.

9. Roll pastry, keeping it as circular as possible, into a 12-inch circle. Invert 9-inch pie plate over pastry. Make a mark 1½ inches from edge of plate all the way around. Cut through mark with sharp knife. Lift off plate.

10. Fold pastry in half. Lift into pie plate. Unfold. Ease pastry into plate so it fits the shape of plate. Do not stretch pastry, as this causes it to shrink during baking.

11. Trim pastry with scissors ½ inch from edge of pie plate. Fold the ½ inch under, even with edge of plate.

12. Press pastry gently with fingers to form a high stand-up rim.

13. Flute edge. Place index finger of one hand firmly on inside of rim, and thumb and index finger of other hand at the same point on outside of rim. Pinch. Repeat all around edge.

14. Prick pastry thoroughly on bottom and sides with tines of fork.

15. Cut a piece of wax paper to fit into pastry shell; place in shell. Fill with raw rice or dried beans. This keeps shell in shape as it bakes.

16. Bake 5 minutes. Remove paper and rice or beans. Bake shell 12 to 15 minutes or until golden brown. Remove from oven. Cool on wire rack.

17. Empty gelatin into bowl. Add boiling water. Stir to dissolve.

18. Add strawberries. Chill until mixture is very thick but not set.

19. Prepare topping mix with cold milk as package directs. Stir in 1 cup of the thickened strawberry mixture.

20. Add remaining strawberry mixture. With a spatula, cut down one side of mixture, across bottom, up the other side and over the top. Turn bowl slightly and repeat. Keep doing this folding until mixtures are completely combined.

21. Chill just until mixture will mound when spooned. Turn into cooled pastry shell. Chill until set.

Rosenblum

CARAMEL APPLE PIE

2 cups sifted all-purpose flour
½ teaspoon salt
¾ cup shortening
6 tablespoons cold water
¼ cup sugar
¾ cup brown sugar, firmly packed
¼ cup all-purpose flour
½ teaspoon ground cinnamon
¼ teaspoon ground nutmeg
⅛ teaspoon salt
¼ cup butter or margarine
6 to 8 medium-size cooking apples
2 teaspoons lemon juice
Milk
Sugar

Prepare pastry with 2 cups flour, ½ teaspoon salt, shortening, and cold water as the first 6 steps of Strawberry Velvet Pie.

Divide pastry in half. Roll out one half a 12-inch circle on a lightly floured board.

Fold pastry in half. Lift into 9-inch pie plate. Unfold. Fit pastry into bottom and sides of plate without stretching.

Mix ¼ cup sugar, brown sugar, ¼ cup flour, cinnamon, nutmeg, and ⅛ teaspoon salt in a small bowl.

Cut in butter or margarine until particles are fine.

6. Cut apples in quarters. Remove cores and skins.

7. Slice apples into large bowl. Sprinkle with lemon juice.

8. Add brown-sugar mixture. Toss gently until apples are coated. Turn into pastry-lined pie plate.

9. Heat oven to 400° F.

10. Roll out remaining half of pastry to 12-inch circle. Fold in half.

11. Cut several slits near center to allow steam to escape during baking and to keep crust from puffing up.

12. Place carefully on apples. Unfold.

13. Fold edge of top pastry under edge of bottom pastry on rim.

14. Pinch with fingers to form a high, standing collar around rim.

15. Flute edge: Place index finger of one hand on inside of rim, thumb and index finger of other hand on outside at the same point. Pinch. Repeat all around the edge. Pinch each one of the flutes again to sharpen points.

16. Brush top of pie with milk. Sprinkle with sugar. This gives your pie a pretty, sparkling crust.

17. Bake 40 to 50 minutes or until pie is golden brown. Remove from oven. Cool on wire rack.

COOKIES

TIPS ON COOKIE BAKING

Here are some things you'll want to know before you begin to make cookies:

- Choose the right cookie sheet. There are three standard sizes available. Select a size that is two inches narrower and two inches shorter than your oven so the heat can circulate around it while the cookies bake.

- If the recipe calls for a greased cookie sheet, coat it lightly with shortening. Spread it evenly with a pastry brush, a piece of wax paper, or paper towel.

- Cookie dough will melt if it is put on a hot cookie sheet, so have a second, cool one for the next batch to be baked. Let the hot cookie sheet cool before you use it again.

- Be careful with flour. Measure accurately for the recipe and don't use too much when you roll the dough. Too much flour will make your cookies tough and dry.

- Make each cookie the same size and thickness for uniform baking.

- Use a broad spatula to pick up rolled cookies from the board. It helps keep them from stretching.

- Remove cookies from the cookie sheets as soon as they come from the oven. Again, transfer them with a broad spatula and place them on wire cake racks in a single layer.

- Don't overlap cookies when placing them on wire rack. This could cause them to stick and lose their shape.

- Avoid overbaking. Remember, cookies continue to bake after they are removed from the oven until they are taken from the cookie sheet.

OLD-FASHIONED SUGAR COOKIES

3½ cups sifted all-purpose flour
2½ teaspoons baking powder
½ teaspoon salt
1 cup soft butter or margarine
1½ cups sugar
2 eggs
3 teaspoons vanilla
Granulated or colored sugar
Butter or margarine

1. Heat oven to 400° F. Grease cookie sheets lightly.

2. Sift flour, baking powder, and salt onto a piece of wax paper.

3. Put 1 cup butter or margarine, 1½ cups sugar, eggs, and vanilla into a medium-size bowl. Beat until light and fluffy.

4. Add the sifted, dry ingredients a small amount at a time, blending thoroughly after each addition.

44

Pinch off a small piece of dough. Roll between palms into a ball about one inch diameter. Place on cookie sheet.

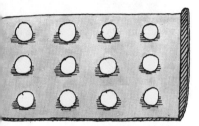

Repeat pinching and rolling dough, placing balls about 2 inches apart on cookie sheet.

Put granulated or colored sugar into small bowl or a 10-ounce custard cup.

Butter bottom of water tumbler lightly.

Dip tumbler in sugar and press balls of dough down carefully until they are about ⅛ inch thick.

Bake 10 to 12 minutes or until edges of cookies are golden brown.

Remove from cookie sheets with spatula and carefully place on wire cake racks. Cool thoroughly. Makes about 4 dozen cookies.

GINGER COOKIES

4½ to 5 cups sifted all-purpose flour
2 teaspoons baking soda
1 teaspoon ground ginger
1 teaspoon ground cinnamon
1 teaspoon ground cloves
¼ teaspoon salt
1 cup butter or margarine
1 cup sugar
1 cup molasses
1 tablespoon vinegar
1 egg, beaten

1. Sift flour, baking soda, ginger, cinnamon, cloves, and salt together. Set aside.

2. Put butter or margarine and sugar into a large bowl.

3. Put molasses into a small saucepan. Heat to boiling.

4. Pour molasses over butter or margarine and sugar. Add vinegar. Stir until well blended. Set aside and let it cool.

5. Add beaten egg to cooled molasses mixture.

6. Add sifted flour mixture gradually, mixing well after each addition.

7. Cover bowl with aluminum foil, wax paper, or transparent plastic wrap. Chill overnight.

8. Heat oven to 375° F. Grease a cookie sheet lightly.

9. Divide dough into four parts. Roll out one part at a time on a well-floured board, rolling from center to the edge. Keep rest of dough in refrigerator while rolling one part.
For soft, fat cookies roll the dough ¼ inch thick. If you want your cookies thin and crisp, roll the dough ⅛ inch thick.

10. Put a small amount of flour in a small bowl. Dip cookie cutter in the flour. Shake off the excess.

11. Cut out cookies, keeping the cuttings close together and cutting as many as you can from each rolling.

12. Pick up cookies one at a time with a broad spatula and place them about 1 inch apart on cookie sheet.

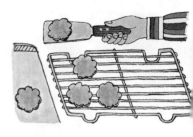

13. Bake 8 to 10 minutes. Remove from oven. Transfer cookies to wire rack with a broad spatula. Don't stack or overlap them. Cool completely.

GINGERBREAD MEN

1 recipe for Ginger Cookies
Raisins
Milk or water
1 cup sifted confectioners' sugar

1. Prepare and chill dough for Ginger Cookies.

2. Roll dough out ¼ inch thick.

3. Cut out with floured gingerbread-man cutter.

4. Transfer to greased cookie sheet with a broad spatula or pancake turner.

5. Press raisins into dough for eyes, nose and mouth.

6. If you wish, move the arms and legs carefully, so the gingerbread men will look as though they are running after they are baked.

7. Bake as for Ginger Cookies.

8. Remove carefully from cookie sheets with broad spatula and place on wire racks to cool.

9. Stir enough milk or water into confectioners' sugar to make an icing easy to force through a pastry tube, yet firm enough to hold its shape. Do it slowly by teaspoonfuls for you may need only a tablespoon of liquid or less.

10. Press through pastry tube in thin lines to make outlines for the collar, cuffs, belt, and shoes.

DESSERTS

APPLE BETTY

6 slices white bread
½ cup butter or margarine
½ cup brown sugar, firmly packed
1 teaspoon ground cinnamon
½ teaspoon ground allspice
6 medium-size apples
⅓ cup water

1. Turn on the oven to 375° F. Grease a 1½-quart baking dish.

2. Cut bread slices into tiny cubes. When done, you should have 3 cups.

3. Melt the butter or margarine and pour it into a large bowl. Add bread cubes and toss with a fork. Measure out ½ cup bread cubes; set aside.

4. Measure the brown sugar. Pack it down firmly so it will hold together when turned out of the cup. Add the sugar to the bread cubes in the bowl.

5. Add the cinnamon and allspice.

6. Cut the apples in quarters. Remove the cores and skin. Slice the apples and put into the bowl with the other ingredients. Add the water and mix together.

7. Spoon the mixture into the greased casserole. Sprinkle the saved ½ cup bread cubes on top.

8. Cover the baking dish. If the dish has no cover of its own fit a piece of aluminum foil over the top of the dish.

9. Put it in the preheated oven and bake 30 minutes. Remove the cover and bake 30 minutes more. Serve warm. Delicious with cream poured over it or with vanilla ice cream. Makes 6 servings.

DUTCH PEACH CAKE

4 medium-size peaches
2 tablespoons lemon juice
1½ cups sifted all-purpose flour
2 teaspoons baking powder
½ teaspoon salt
¼ cup sugar
½ cup shortening
1 egg
½ cup milk
1 teaspoon ground cinnamon
¼ cup melted butter or margarine
Vanilla Sauce

1. Heat oven to 400° F. Grease 11x7×inch pan or baking dish.

2. Put peaches in bowl. Cover with b‹ing water. Let stand 1 to 2 minutes.

3. Transfer peaches with slotted spoon to a bowl of cold water.

4. Peel and slice peaches thinly. Sprinkle with lemon juice to keep from darkening.

5. Sift flour, baking powder, salt, and ¼ cup sugar into a bowl.

6. Cut in shortening with pastry blender until mixture resembles cornmeal.

7. Beat egg and milk together. Add to flour mixture. Stir just until dough is blended.

8. Spread dough in prepared pan.

9. Press peach slices into dough in rows, overlapping them slightly.

10. Mix ¼ cup sugar and cinnamon. Sprinkle over peaches.

11. Drizzle top with butter or margarine.

12. Bake 30 to 35 minutes or until cake tester inserted in center comes out clean.

13. Cut in squares. Serve warm with Vanilla Sauce. Makes 9 squares.

CUSTARDS

Custards are mixtures of milk, eggs, salt, sweetening, and flavoring. A soft custard is cooked in a double boiler over hot water and stirred constantly. Soft custard is especially good served over fruit—fresh, cooked, or canned; and over whipped gelatin desserts or steamed puddings. Firm custards may be baked or steamed. As with all egg cookery, care must be taken not to overcook custards.

5. Remove top of double boiler and set in a bowl or pan of cold water to cool custard quickly, or pour custard into a cool bowl immediately.

6. Cool custard. Stir in vanilla. Cover and refrigerate. Makes 6 servings.

SOFT CUSTARD

2 cups milk
3 eggs
¼ cup sugar
¼ teaspoon salt
1 teaspoon vanilla

1. Heat milk in top of double boiler until tiny bubbles appear around the edge. Remove from heat. This is the test for scalded milk.

2. Beat eggs in a medium-size bowl just until they are blended. Stir in sugar and salt.

3. Add hot milk very slowly, stirring constantly. Pour into top of double boiler.

4. Set over (not in) hot, not boiling, water in bottom of double boiler. Cook, stirring constantly, until custard is thick enough to coat the spoon with a thin film. Remove from heat at once.

GOLDEN BAKED CUSTARD

2 cups milk
2 eggs
½ cup sugar
¼ teaspoon salt
1 teaspoon vanilla

1. Heat oven to 350° F.

2. Heat milk in saucepan just until bubbles appear around the edge. Remove from heat.

3. Beat eggs in medium-size bowl just until they are blended. Stir in sugar and salt.

4. Add hot milk very slowly, stirring constantly. Stir in vanilla.

5. Pour into 1½-quart baking dish. Set dish in larger pan. Place on oven rack. If you like the flavor of nutmeg you can sprinkle the top of your custard with ground nutmeg at this point.

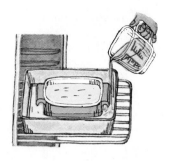

6. Pour hot water into larger pan until level of water is even with level of custard in baking dish. This is a most important step in baking custard. The water bath protects the custard during baking and helps to keep it from overcooking. You may have seen a baked custard in which the bottom portion was smooth and velvety and the top inch or so was full of tiny holes or bubbles. The levels of water and custard should be the same so all the custard is protected and this bubbly appearance will be avoided.

7. Bake 40 to 45 minutes or until a thin-bladed knife inserted 1 inch from the edge comes out clean. The center will be soft but will set as the custard cools because the eggs will continue to cook. Remove from oven. Cool. Chill. Makes 6 servings.

Note: Custard may be baked in 6 custard cups and served in them, or may be unmolded after being chilled.

OLD-FASHIONED RICE PUDDING

1 quart (4 cups) milk
¼ cup sugar
¼ cup raw long-grain rice
1 tablespoon butter or margarine
¼ teaspoon salt
¼ teaspoon ground nutmeg
1 teaspoon vanilla
½ cup raisins (optional)

1. Heat oven to 325° F.

2. Grease a 1½-quart casserole. Combine milk, sugar, rice, butter or margarine, salt, nutmeg, and vanilla in the casserole.

3. Bake pudding uncovered, 2 hours, stirring often.

4. Add raisins. Stir gently. Bake 30 minutes longer or until rice is very tender. Serve warm or cold. Makes 6 servings.

CREAM PUFFS

1 cup sifted all-purpose flour
1 cup water
½ cup butter or margarine
⅛ teaspoon salt
4 eggs

1. Heat oven to 400° F.

2. Sift and measure flour. Set aside.

3. Put water, butter or margarine, and salt in saucepan. Bring to boiling over high heat, stirring occasionally. Butter or margarine will be melted.

4 Lower heat. Add flour all at once and stir rapidly until mixture forms a ball and follows spoon around the pan. Remove from heat. Cool slightly.

5. Add 1 egg. Beat well until mixture is smooth and egg is blended in. Repeat with remaining 3 eggs, adding them one at a time and beating until each is blended in before adding the next one. Mixture will be slippery and separated, but the beating will make it smooth.

6. Drop from spoon onto ungreased cookie sheet in 12 even mounds, placing mounds about 3 inches apart. Use a rubber spatula to help push mixture off spoon

a cream puff is a heavenly dessert. Have you ever eaten one and wondered how the delicate, crisp, hollow shell was made? These French creations are really one of the easiest and simplest desserts to make.

The dough for making cream puffs is called "paté a chou" and it is the same dough used for making eclairs and other fabulous desserts. So once you learn to make it you can go on to become a pastry cook of distinction.

Cream puffs depend on steam to make them puff and they must go into a hot oven to puff immediately—so the oven must be preheated. They will puff four to five times their original size, so be sure you space them far apart on the cookie sheet. Bake the puffs until they are brown and dry. A puff that is still moist inside will collapse. Follow the recipe directions for beating and mixing so your dough is smooth and glossy and will hold its shape.

Cream puffs may be filled with pastry cream and topped with glaze as we have done or they may be filled with ice cream or sweetened whipped cream and the tops dusted with confectioners' sugar. Ice-cream-filled ones may also be served with a sundae sauce. Tiny puffs made from the same dough, filled, served with chocolate sauce, become a special dessert—Chocolate Profiteroles. Cream puffs are versatile—serve them a different way each time.

Bake puffs 45 to 50 minutes or until ‑y are puffed and brown and there are tiny bubbles of moisture on the sur‑ e. Remove from oven.

Transfer puffs from cookie sheet to e racks with spatula. Cool them, away m drafts, while you make pastry cream.

Cut tops from puffs with a sharp knife. move any pieces of soft dough from centers.

PASTRY CREAM

½ cup sifted all-purpose flour
½ cup sugar
¼ teaspoon salt
2 cups milk
3 eggs
1½ teaspoons vanilla
1 teaspoon butter or margarine
½ cup heavy cream

1. Put flour, sugar, and salt into medium-size saucepan. Mix thoroughly.

2. Add milk slowly, stirring to blend and keep mixture smooth.

3. Place saucepan over medium heat. Cook, stirring constantly, until mixture is thickened and bubbly. Cook 2 minutes. Remove from heat.

4. Beat eggs slightly in small bowl. Add half the hot milk-flour mixture slowly, stirring constantly.

5. Pour egg mixture back into saucepan. Cook over medium heat, stirring constantly, 1 minute or until mixture is bubbly. Remove from heat.

6. Stir in vanilla and butter or margarine. Place a piece of wax paper right on top of the hot pastry cream to prevent a skin from forming on the top. Cool.

7. Whip cream in small bowl until stiff. Fold into pastry cream using a rubber spatula and an up-and-over motion until mixtures are blended. Chill until ready to fill puffs.

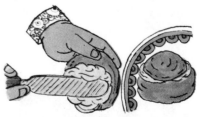

8. Fill puffs. Replace tops. Refrigerate. Just before serving, make Chocolate Glaze and spoon over tops.

CHOCOLATE GLAZE

2 squares unsweetened chocolate
1 teaspoon butter or margarine
1 cup sifted confectioners' sugar
3 tablespoons water

1. Put chocolate and butter or margarine in top of double boiler. Place over hot water in bottom of double boiler. Heat until melted. Stir to blend.

2. Add confectioners' sugar. Stir in until completely blended.

3. Add water. Beat until mixture is smooth.

4. Spoon glaze over tops of cream puffs at once.

STRAWBERRY CLOUD

1 package
(3 ounces) strawberry gelatin
1 cup boiling water
1 cup cold water
1 pint strawberries
1 egg white
2 tablespoons sugar

1. Empty gelatin mix into a bowl.

2. Add the boiling water. Stir until gelatin is dissolved. Stir in the cold water.

3. Chill until gelatin is thick and syrupy. It should have a consistency like that of honey when you spoon it.

4. Wash, hull, and slice strawberries.

Set the bowl of syrupy gelatin in a
ger bowl with ice. Add the egg white.

Beat with egg beater until mixture is
t and fluffy.

Add 1 cup sliced strawberries. Pour
o 6-cup mold. Chill until firm.

Sprinkle remaining strawberries with
gar. Chill.

9. To unmold gelatin: Dip mold into warm
(not hot) water just until water reaches
level of gelatin. Remove quickly.

10. Run tip of small spatula between
gelatin and mold.

11. Place large plate on top of mold.
Turn over quickly. Shake gently, holding
dish tightly to mold. Lift off mold. Serve
with sweetened strawberries. Top with
whipped cream, if desired.

CONFECTIONS

TIPS ON
CANDY MAKING

Make candy on a cool, dry day for best results. Candy made on a damp day may be sugary.

The best and most accurate way to test candy when cooking it, is with a candy thermometer. Here's how to use it:

1. Clip the thermometer on the side of the saucepan before starting to cook and leave it in the mixture all during cooking.

2. Be sure the bulb is completely covered with syrup—not just with the boiling foam. Do not let the thermometer rest on the bottom of the saucepan.

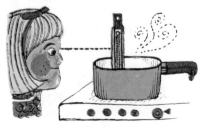

3 To read the thermometer correctly, your eyes should be on a level with the mercury. Bend down so they are—do take the thermometer out of the syr to read it.

4 When candy has finished cookin remove the thermometer and let it cc before washing it.

PEANUT BRITTLE

1 pound shelled peanuts
3 cups sugar
1¼ cups water
½ cup light corn syrup
3 tablespoons butter or margarine
1 teaspoon baking soda
1 tablespoon water
1½ teaspoons vanilla

1. Butter a large cookie sheet.

2. If peanuts are salted, rinse in wa water. Dry well with paper towels.

3. Combine sugar, water, and corn syr in heavy saucepan. Clip candy thermo eter on side of pan.

4. Cook over medium heat, stirring co stantly, until sugar is dissolved and m ture comes to boiling.

56

Let mixture boil without stirring until candy thermometer registers 270° F.

Remove pan from heat. Add butter margarine and peanuts.

Continue cooking candy until thermometer registers 300° F. Remove the pan from heat.

Mix soda and water.

Add soda mixture and vanilla to hot candy. Let bubbles subside.

Pour, as thinly as possible, onto prepared pan. Cool.

Break peanut brittle into pieces. Makes about 2¾ pounds.

CHOCOLATE CHERRIES

1 jar (8 ounces) stemmed maraschino
cherries
5 squares semi-sweet (candy-making)
chocolate

1. Put a large piece of wax paper on a cookie sheet.

2. Drain the juice from the cherries.

3. Put the chocolate squares in the top of a small double boiler. Place over hot, not boiling water. Heat until melted.

4. Hold a cherry firmly by the stem and dip into the chocolate to coat it.

5. Place it on the wax paper. Repeat with rest of the cherries. Let set until chocolate hardens. Makes 2 dozen.

8 cups popped popcorn
1 cup light corn syrup
1 cup sugar
¼ cup water
1 teaspoon vinegar
Red or green food coloring
2 tablespoons butter or margarine
1 teaspoon vanilla

1. Put popcorn into large bowl.

2. Mix corn syrup, sugar, water, and vinegar in saucepan.

3. Add red or green food coloring, a drop at a time, to tint mixture a bright pink or green. If you have one of those squeeze-type bottles, do it right over the syrup. Otherwise drop it from the teaspoon. Clip candy thermometer to side of pan.

4. Cook over medium heat, stirring constantly, until sugar dissolves.

5. Cook, without stirring, until candy thermometer registers 260° F.

6. Add butter or margarine and vanilla.

7. Pour over popcorn. Stir mixtu quickly with spoon or fork so all litt pieces of popcorn are coated with syru

8. Butter palms of hands. Scoop portion of popcorn mixture. Press ve *lightly* into ball. Drop on wax paper.

9. Continue shaping balls, working ra idly and buttering your hands as neede Makes 9 large or 18 small balls.

10. For garland, string balls on th strong cord, using a heavy, large- ey needle. Tie bows on ends.

WALNUT BUTTERSCOTCH CANDY BALLS

packages (6 ounces each) butterscotch-
flavored pieces
1 can (14–15 ounces) sweetened
condensed milk
4 cups cornflakes
2 cups chopped walnuts
½ cup raisins
½ cup chopped, drained maraschino
cherries
1¼ cups finely chopped walnuts

Put butterscotch pieces into top of
2-quart double boiler. Place over hot
water in bottom of double boiler and heat
until butterscotch pieces are melted.

Blend in condensed milk.

3. Stir in cornflakes, 2 cups chopped walnuts, the raisins, and the cherries.

4. Spread the finely chopped walnuts on
a piece of wax paper for coating.

5. Shape about a teaspoonful of the butterscotch mixture into a small ball. Roll in
nuts to coat. Place on a cookie sheet or
flat pan. Repeat with the rest of the butterscotch mixture. Chill until it is firm.
This makes about 5 dozen.

PEANUT BUTTER FUDGE

⅓ cup butter or margarine
½ cup corn syrup
¾ cup peanut butter (cream-style
or chunky)
½ teaspoon salt
1 teaspoon vanilla
4½ cups sifted confectioners'
sugar
¾ cup chopped walnuts or pecans

1. Put butter or margarine in large bowl. Press against sides of bowl with back of wooden spoon until soft.

2. Blend in corn syrup, peanut butter, salt, and vanilla. Mix until creamy.

3. Stir in confectioners' sugar gradually, mixing until smooth.

4. Turn fudge out on a board. Knead wit hands until blended and smooth.
5. Add nuts gradually, pressing an kneading them into the candy.
6. Press candy out to a ½-inch-thic square with your hands or a rolling pi Cut in squares. Makes about 2 pound

NUT MINTS

1¼ cups sifted confectioners' sugar
¼ cup sweetened condensed milk
¼ teaspoon peppermint extract
Few drops red food coloring
Few drops green food coloring
Walnut or pecan halves

1. Put confectioners' sugar into a m dium-size bowl. Blend in condensed mi
2. Add peppermint extract. Beat wi wooden spoon until smooth and cream
3. Take half the mixture and put it into second bowl for adding food colorir

. Tint one half of the mixture a delicate pink with red food coloring. Mix it in very slowly, drop by drop, until your candy is the color you want.

. Tint the other half a delicate green with green food coloring.

. Take about a teaspoonful at a time and roll it into a small ball between the palms of your hands that you have first dusted with confectioners' sugar. Place the balls on wax paper far enough apart for pressing down.

Flatten each ball with the bottom of a glass. Top each mint patty with a walnut or pecan half. Makes about 2 dozen.

SPICED NUTS

¾ cup sugar
2 teaspoons ground cinnamon
¼ teaspoon ground cloves
¼ teaspoon ground nutmeg
1 egg white
2 tablespoons water
1½ cups walnut halves
1½ cups pecan halves

1. Heat oven to 250° F.

2. Sift sugar, cinnamon, cloves, and nutmeg into shallow dish (a pie plate is good to use).

3. Beat egg white and water slightly in bowl.

4. Add walnuts and pecans to egg mixture, about ½ cup at a time. Stir with fork until well moistened. Lift out, letting excess syrup drain off.

5. Toss nuts in sugar mixture until well coated.

6. Place nuts, spread out, on greased cookie sheets.

7. Bake 40 minutes or until crusty. Cool. Makes 3 cups.

APRICOT-PINEAPPLE JAM

1 package (8 ounces) dried apricots
Six 8-ounce jelly glasses with lids
1 can (1 pound, 14 ounces) crushed
pineapple, drained
1 small lemon, thinly sliced
4 cups sugar

1. Wash apricots. Put in bowl. Soak overnight.

2. Wash glasses and lids in hot, soapy water. Rinse. Put in large kettle. Cover with water. Bring to boiling; boil 10 minutes. Turn off heat. Leave glasses and lids in water until ready to fill. Re-

move from kettle with tongs. Invert on towels to drain. Glasses should be hot and dry when filled.

3. Simmer apricots, in water in which they were soaked, until tender.

4. Mash apricots. Add pineapple, lemon, and sugar.

5. Simmer, stirring often, until jam is thick and clear. Remove lemon slices.

6. Pour into hot, sterilized glasses. Seal while hot.

TO SEAL WITH PARAFFIN: Remove jam from heat. Stir and skim for 5 minutes to cool slightly and prevent floating fruit in jam. Ladle into glasses quickly, leaving ½-inch space at top. Cover at once with ⅛-inch-thick layer of melted paraffin. Cool. Cover glasses with lids. Label. Store in cool place.

TO SEAL WITHOUT PARAFFIN: Use glasses or jars with two-piece metal lids. Remove jam from heat. With metal spoon, quickly skim off foam. Ladle boiling hot jam into jars or glasses, leaving ⅛-inch space at top. Place lid on jar, screw band on tightly, and invert jar. Repeat with remaining jars. When all jars are filled, turn them upright. Cool. Shake gently after one-half hour to keep fruit from floating. Label. Store in cool place.

TABLE OF
EQUIVALENT WEIGHTS AND MEASURES

Dash (liquid)	=	Few drops
Dash (dry)	=	Less than ⅛ teaspoon
3 teaspoons	=	1 tablespoon
1½ teaspoons	=	½ tablespoon
4 tablespoons	=	¼ cup
5 tablespoons +1 teaspoon	=	⅓ cup
8 tablespoons	=	½ cup
10 tablespoons +2 teaspoons	=	⅔ cup
12 tablespoons	=	¾ cup
16 tablespoons	=	1 cup
2 cups	=	1 pint
4 cups (2 pints)	=	1 quart
4 quarts (liquid)	=	1 gallon
8 quarts (dry)	=	1 peck
4 pecks	=	1 bushel
1 fluid ounce	=	2 tablespoons
8 fluid ounces	=	1 cup
32 fluid ounces	=	1 quart
25 fluid ounces	=	1 fifth (of gallon)

TABLE OF FOOD EQUIVALENTS

Butter or Margarine
¼ pound = ½ cup
½ pound = 1 cup
Note: Measurement of whipped butter
or margarine is greater.

Cream
Heavy cream, ½ pint
(1 cup) = 2 cups whipped

Cheese
Cream cheese,
8-ounce package = 1 cup
Cottage cheese,
½-pound carton = 1 cup
Grated process American
or Cheddar, ¼ pound = 1 cup
½ pound = 2 cups

Flour and Meal
All-purpose flour, 1 pound = 4 cups sifted
Cake flour, 1 pound = 4½ to 5 cups
sifted
Cornmeal, 1 pound = 3 cups

Sugar
Granulated, 1 pound = 2¼ to 2½ cups
Superfine, 1 pound = 2⅓ cups
Confectioners' sugar,
1 pound = Approximately
4 cups, unsifted
4½ to 5 cups
sifted
Light brown, 1 pound = 2⅓ cups,
firmly packed
Dark brown, 1 pound = 2⅛ to 2¼ cups,
firmly packed

Fruit
Apples, 1 pound = 3 medium
(3 cups sliced)
1 medium, chopped = 1 cup
Bananas, 1 pound 3 medium
(2½ cups sliced)

Strawberries, 1 quart = 3½ cups hulled
Lemon juice,
1 medium lemon = 3 tablespoons
Lemon rind grated,
1 medium lemon = 1 tablespoon
Orange juice,
1 medium orange = ⅓ to ½ cup
Orange rind grated,
1 medium orange = 2 tablespoons
Dates, pitted,
8-ounce package = 1¾ cups, cut up
Raisins, seedless,
15-ounce package = 3 cups

Vegetables

Onions, 1 pound yellow = 5 or 6 medium,
3 large
1 pound small white = 12 to 14
1 medium, chopped = ½ cup
Potatoes, 1 pound white = 3 medium
(2⅓ to 2½
cups sliced)
1 pound sweet = 3 medium
(2½ to 3
cups sliced)
Green beans, 1 pound = 3 cups cut

Nuts (1 pound)	In Shell	Shelled
Almond	1 to 1¾ cups nutmeats	3½ cups nutmeats
Peanuts	2 to 2¼ cups nutmeats	3 cups nutmeats
Pecans	2¼ cups nutmeats	4 cups nutmeats
Walnuts	1⅔ cups nutmeats	4 cups nutmeats

Pasta

Macaroni, elbow, 8 ounces = 2 cups uncooked
4 cups cooked

Spaghetti (1½-inch
pieces), 8 ounces = 2 cups uncooked
4 cups cooked

Noodles, 8 ounces = About 3 cups
uncooked, 3¾
cups cooked

HOW TO MAKE SUBSTITUTIONS

INSTEAD OF	USE
1 tablespoon cornstarch, potato starch, or arrowroot (as thickening)	2 tablespoons flour
1 cup fresh sweet milk	⅓ cup instant non-fat dry milk plus 1 cup water and 2½ teaspoons butter or margarine; or ½ cup evaporated milk plus ½ cup water
1 cup buttermilk or sour milk	1 tablespoon lemon juice or vinegar plus enough sweet milk to make 1 cup (let stand 5 minutes)
1 cup honey	¾ cup sugar plus ¼ cup liquid
1 cup corn syrup	¾ cup sugar plus ¼ cup liquid
1 square (1 ounce) unsweetened chocolate	3 tablespoons cocoa plus 1 tablespoon butter or margarine; or 1-ounce package unsweetened chocolate-flavored baking product
2 egg yolks	1 whole egg
1 medium-size onion, chopped	1 tablespoon instant minced onion, rehydrated

COMMON CONTAINER SIZES

Labels on cans or jars of identical size may show a net weight for one product that differs slightly from the net weight of another due to the differences in the density of the foods. An example would be baked beans (1 lb.) and blueberries (14-oz.) in the same size can.

Industry Term	Approx. Net Weight or Fluid Measure (check label)	Approx. Cups	Principal Products
	Consumer Description		
8 oz.	8 oz.	1	Fruits, vegetables, specialties* for small families. 2 servings.
Picnic	10½ to 12 oz.	1¼	Mainly condensed soups. Some fruits, vegetables, meat, fish, specialties.* 3 servings.
12 oz. (vacuum)	12 oz.	1½	Principally for vacuum-pack corn. 3 to 4 servings.
No. 300	14 to 16 oz.	1¾	Pork and beans, baked beans, meat products, cranberry sauce, blueberries, specialties.* 3 to 4 servings.
No. 303	16 to 17 oz.	2	Principal size for fruits and vegetables. Some meat products, ready-to-serve soups, specialties.* 4 servings.
No. 2	1 lb. 4 oz. or 1 pt. 2 fl. oz.	2½	Juices, ready-to-serve soups, some specialties,* pineapple, apple slices. No longer in popular use for most fruits and vegetables. 5 servings.
No. 2½	1 lb. 13 oz.	3½	Fruits, some vegetables (pumpkin, sauerkraut, spinach and other greens, tomatoes). 7 servings.
No. 3 cyl. or 46 fl. oz.	3 lb. 3 oz. or 1 qt. 14 fl. oz.	5¾	"Economy family size" fruit and vegetable juices, pork and beans. Institutional size for condensed soups, some vegetables. 10 to 12 servings.
No. 10	6½ lb. to 7 lb. 5 oz.	12–13	Institutional size for fruits, vegetables, and some other foods. 25 servings.

Meats, fish, and seafood are almost entirely advertised and sold under weight terminology.

Infant and junior foods come in small cans and jars suitable for the smaller servings used. Content is given on label.

Specialties—Food combinations prepared by special manufacturers' recipes.

NOTES